ESCARPMENT
TRAILS AND TREKS

TWO-HOUR HIKES IN HALTON, HAMILTON AND NIAGARA

CHRIS PARR
SHARON TKACZ

Tellwell Talent
www.tellwell.ca

ISBN
978-1-7781041-0-7 (Paperback)
978-0-2288-8004-2 (eBook)

CONTENTS

HALTON

HAMILTON

NIAGARA

This book is dedicated to our hiking leaders
for introducing us to these trails and treks,
and to our amazing group of hiking friends:

André
Angela
Carmen
Carol
Cherie
Chris
Daljeet
Jim
Karen
Martin
Randy
Roma
Sharon
Wolfgang

Coyote

We would also like to acknowledge that these hiking trails are on the traditional territory of the Anishinaabe, Hatiwendaronk, and Haudenosaunee peoples, including the Mississaugas of the Credit First Nation, many of whom continue to live and work here today. This territory is covered by the Upper Canada Treaties, and the Haldimand Treaty is within the lands protected by the Dish with One Spoon Wampum Agreement.

We are privileged to be able to traverse these lands. We encourage all hikers to treat them with gratitude and respect.

Red Admiral

Scarlet Tanager

"Hiking is a bit like life. The journey only requires you to put one foot in front of the other . . . again, and again, and again. And if you allow yourself opportunity to be present throughout the entirety of the trek, you will witness beauty every step of the way, not just at the summit."

– Unknown

Introducing The Hikers Dozen

The Hikers Dozen is like a baker's dozen. We are an eclectic group of twelve people, with the occasional extra hiker thrown into the mix. We came together by chance, responding to a gathering at the Chedoke Radial Trail on Monday mornings to hike the Bruce Trail under the leadership of Daljeet. As the group became more regular, and with the additional impetus of COVID, we decided to add some different and more adventurous hikes on Fridays. We came together because of our love for the land, an appreciation for nature, and that shared

Chedoke West Hike

feeling of exhilaration when we make it to the top of a steep, rocky hill to an expansive lookout over the escarpment or lake. Mud, puddles, slippery rocks, ice, even insects have not deterred our stalwart hiking time together! No matter the circumstances, twice a week The Hikers Dozen gathers to hike.

Throughout COVID, our times together sustained us (when not curtailed by gathering restrictions). We supported each other through cancer treatments, worries about children, siblings and elderly parents. We discussed the challenges of the world and solved them all! Or we were silent and reflective as we experienced the sanctity of nature. Often our hikes took us to a destination such as a dam, a waterfall (or several), or a lake. We continue to be grateful for the abundance of nature that surrounds us.

"The land is the real teacher. All we need as students is mindfulness."
– Robin Wall Kimmerer, <u>Braiding Sweetgrass: Indigenous Wisdom, Scientific</u>
<u>Knowledge and the Teachings of Plants</u>

Why this book?

We are often asked by friends and family to recommend a hike for themselves or visiting relatives. The Halton, Hamilton and Niagara region is a hiker's paradise. In addition to the Bruce Trail, there are many conservation areas, waterfalls, and local trails to be discovered. Many of our hikes feature beautiful wildflowers in the spring and summer, stunning fall colours in the autumn months, and equally scenic and accessible trails in the winter. We have found that visiting hikers prefer trails that are long enough for a cardio workout but do not take a day to accomplish. While there are many great hiking books, it is usually necessary to search for a hike that is neither too long nor too short. This book identifies hikes that average two hours in duration and seven kilometers in distance, hiking at a moderate pace. We consider them "just-right hikes."

The purpose of this book is to highlight some especially beautiful trails for hikers both new and experienced. In addition, it highlights great points of interest to explore. We want to share our enthusiasm for communing with nature and the wellbeing it offers. Hiking could well be the answer to nurturing positive mental health and developing resilience. We hope you fall in love with this activity and find it as rewarding as we do. Enjoy!

Inquisitive Coyote

GLOSSARY AND GUIDE

Consider:

We have not identified whether a hike is advanced or difficult. A hiker's experience, fitness level, the weather, and trail conditions as well as other factors make it hard to predict what a person may find easy or difficult. Instead, we have endeavoured to describe the terrain and possible conditions to consider. Many of our hikes use the Bruce Trail, as well as the Royal Botanical Gardens and conservation lands in the Halton, Hamilton, and Niagara area in addition to locally developed trails. More information about these organizations and trail systems can be found on their websites.

The Bruce Trail is typically rocky, travels along steep cliffs, and has dirt paths with bare tree roots. It will be marked with white or blue markers to indicate direction. A single white blaze indicates the path is straight ahead. A double blaze of any colour indicates a change in direction. A double blaze is indicated by two parallel marks, with one marking lower than the other. The higher mark indicates the direction the path turns, as seen below:

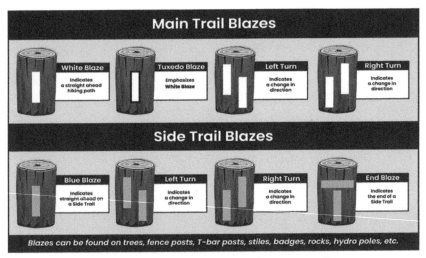

White blazes indicate the Main Bruce Trail.
Blue blazes indicate a side trail (sometimes named).

Terms:

Access Road: An unpaved restricted road, not for regular traffic.

Continue: The term used to indicate there is some distance between instructions or until the next step. These distances vary.

Family Hike: Suitable for children aged eight and up; not "stroller friendly". Strollers are not recommended for any of these hikes.

Intersection: Two trails crossing or meeting at one place; this can be a cross, an X, or a T.

Multi-trail Intersection: More than two trails crossing or meeting.

RBG: The initials for Royal Botanical Gardens, a series of gardens and forested areas located in Burlington and Hamilton. The RBG's resources are devoted to the study and conservation of plants and natural lands of hiking, walking, and experiencing plant species diversity.

Split: One trail splits in two directions, and the hiker will be directed right or left.

Stile: A ladder or narrow fence opening that provides passage of people.

Unmarked Trail: A trail with no markings to give it a name. They are usually well-travelled trails made by local hikers or bikers in the area. Many of the unmarked trails are narrow.

White-Tailed Deer

"There is no such thing as bad weather, only inappropriate clothing."
– Sir Ranulf Fiennes

Words of Wisdom from The Hikers Dozen:

Safety and comfort are very important when hiking; therefore, good hiking equipment is essential. Ensure you are wearing hiking boots that are comfortable and keep your foot and ankle stable and dry. Do not hike in sandals or running shoes. Keep in mind that the trails can be hilly or have steep, long hills to climb.

The following is a list of items you should consider having when hiking:

- **Cell Phone:** ensure your phone is fully charged before hiking
- **Hiking App:** we suggest using an app that tracks your hike and your location, and using the "Find a Friend" or "what3words" app when hiking alone. Both can assist people in finding you in case of an accident.
- **Hiking Boots:** good quality, preferably waterproof
- **Hiking Gaiters:** used over your pants and top of your boots to keep ankles and lower legs dry; they are not necessary, but can be helpful with deep snow and muddy hikes
- **Hiking Poles:** for those requiring help with stability, or with their backs and knees
- **Hiking Socks:** these are a heavier weight with a cushion sole, found at hiking stores, consider "Smart Wool Socks"
- **Icers or Crampons:** these are a must for winter hiking; we suggest Kahtoola MICROspikes ice cleats or Hillsound Trail Crampons; these can be found online, through MEC, Sail, or any hiking store
- **Identification:** in a pocket or knapsack
- **Water Bottle:** for hydration
- **Whistle:** used for signalling when someone has fallen, or help is needed

Recommendations:

After a good hike we have found stopping to have a coffee or other refreshments a welcome reward. We often used this time to plan the next adventure.

The following are suggested locations to share refreshments:

Ball's Falls, Beamer Falls:
Conversations Café: 4995 King Street, Lincoln

Canyon Road, Halton Regional Forest:
The Trail Eatery: 35 Crawford Cres, Campbellville

Chedoke Hikes:
The Lancaster Eatery: Chedoke Golf Club clubhouse, Beddoe Drive, Hamilton
The West Town: 214 Locke Street South, Hamilton

Cootes Paradise South Shore:
Mikel Coffee: 1010 King Street West, Hamilton

Dundas Peak, Christie Lake Crooks' Hollow, Webster Falls:
Collins Brewhouse: 33 King Street West, Dundas
Detour Café: 41 King Street West, Dundas

Fisher's Pond, River and Ruin, Twiss Road:
Luk's Diner: 2501 Guelph Line, Burlington

Cedar Waxwing

Disclaimer

This book is meant as a guide to assist fellow outdoor enthusiasts choose and plan their hikes. It cannot guarantee your safety on the trails. You hike at your own risk, and we assume no liability for any property loss or damage, personal injury, or death that may result from accessing or hiking any trails described in this book.

All participants must assume responsibility for their own actions and safety, exercise sound judgment, be prepared for all conditions, and seek advice on current weather and trail conditions. These conditions change from day to day and from season to season; therefore, information in this book is subject to change without warning.

View from the Beamer Falls Lookout

Webster Falls

Quick Reference

	Pay Parking	Waterfall	Additional Features	Family Hike (8 & up)	Public Washrooms
Ball's Falls		~	^	*	
Beamer Falls		~			
Borer's Falls		~			
Canyon Road				*	
Chedoke East		~			
Chedoke West		~		*	
Christie M.R.	$	~	^	*	w
Christie C.H.	$	~	^	*	w
City View		~		*	w
Cootes NS	$		^	*	w
Cootes SS	$		^	*	
Creek Side			^	*	w
Devil's P/bowl		~	^		w
Dundas Peak		~			w
Fisher's Pond					
Halton Forest		~		*	
Hidden Valley		~			w
McCormack				*	
River & Ruin		~	^	*	
Snake Road			^		
Spring Valley			^	*	
Three W/falls		~		*	
Twiss Road				*	
Webster Falls	$	~	^	*	

Watchful Buck

Spring Trillium

Features and Information

The destination for this hike is Smokey Hollow Falls in Waterdown. In the 1800s, the falls were used to power a local sawmill, turning the area into an industrial centre. As chimneys belched smoke and steam, the valley became known as Smokey Hollow. The waterfall is also known as Grindstone, Waterdown or Great Falls. It is a 10-metre high, fast-flowing ribbon waterfall from Grindstone Creek. Along the hike route are views of Lake Ontario and Kerncliff Park, a former quarry.

Views from the Edge:

Smokey Hollow Falls

Distance
9 km

Terrain
Mainly flat, partly rocky, one steep hill, short residential section

Location and Parking
City View Park, South Parking Lot
2500 Kerns Road, Burlington, L7P 1P8

The south lot is the second entrance south of Dundas Street.

Summary of Hike
This is an out-and-back hike using the Bruce Trail and marked side trails.

1. From the parking lot, follow the blue blazes across the field. At the intersection, turn right and keep right, following blue blazes until meeting the Bruce Trail white blazes.

2. Continue following the white blazes for the remainder of the hike, crossing Kerns Road and King Road, avoiding any blue or unmarked side trails.

3. After the second ladder stile (residential area), the white blazes continue along Flanders Drive. Turn left on Renwood Place, keep left at the dead end, and follow the blazes back into the woods, continuing to the next road.

4. At Mill Street, cross over to the break in the guard rail (use caution crossing the road). Walk down the

hill to the falls. Viewing platform is on the right. This is the turnaround point.

5. Retrace the route to City View Park following the white blazes to the intersection with the side trail; keep left with the blue blazes to return to the field and through to the parking lot.

Option

A short distance after crossing Kerns Road and before meeting the blue blazes, there are small paths on the right leading to a lookout path along the escarpment edge, providing wide panoramic views of Lake Ontario and Kerncliff Park. Follow the railed path to enjoy the views, then return to the marked trails and the field to retrace the route to the parking lot.

Route Map

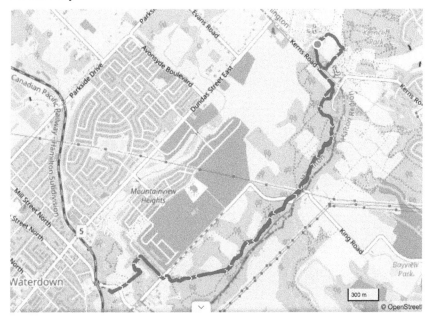

Features and Information

The RBG trails are part of the Hendrie Valley Nature Sanctuary and Lamb's Hollow Wetland; they connect to Hendrie Park, Cherry Hill Gate and Laking Garden. The wetlands and marshes are popular for birdwatching and salmon-spawning in Grindstone Creek. This can be a family-friendly hike. Birds may land on outstretched hands; swans, frogs, and turtles are plentiful; and chipmunks seem to enjoy children's gentle attention. The splash pad and playground at Hidden Valley Park are also well used by families.

The Marsh

Creek Side Boardwalk

Distance
8 km

Terrain
Mainly flat, wide trails, easy footing, few steep sections, boardwalks, stairs.

The Creek Side sections stay very muddy following rain or spring melt.

Location and Parking
Hidden Valley Park parking lots
1137 Hidden Valley Rd, Burlington, L7P 0T5

South parking at sign for Picnic Areas 4–6 (Lemonville Rd, after baseball diamond).

North parking lot at entrance near park facilities.

Summary of Hike
This is an out-and-back hike through Hendrie Valley. RBG trails are named and signs are posted.

1. The hike starts on the Multi-Use Trail at the signs pointing to Royal Botanical Gardens. From the south lot cross the footbridge over the creek, and from the north lot cross the road, turn left on the sidewalk to the start of this trail. Follow the trail along the creek and cross over Unsworth Ave to the RBG entrance.

2. At the sign for Creek Side Walk, follow the trail and continue to an intersection with trail markings and a marsh area on the left.

3. At the intersection, turn left onto Bridle Trail South, passing the marsh lookout and follow Bridle Trail South, turning right into the woods.

4. At the intersection with the bridge on the right, cross the bridge over the creek then turn left at the boardwalk onto Grindstone Marshes Trail. Continue to Spring Garden Road (the trailhead near Laking Garden). This is the turnaround point.

5. Retrace the route on Grindstone Marshes Trail as far as the bridge and boardwalk intersection, then keep left to Bridle Trail North (stairs going up).

6. Continue following Bridle Trail North. After crossing the creek, keep left to the Creek Side Walk Trail. Retrace the route to Unsworth Ave.

7. Cross the road to the Multi-Use Trail and continue to parking lot.

Route Map

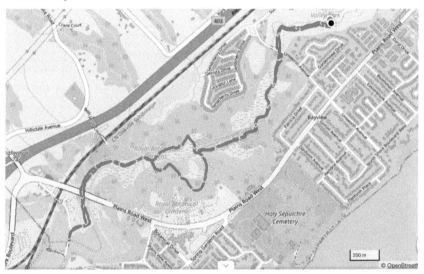

Features and Information

Fisher's Pond Nature Reserve is an 87-acre oasis on the Niagara Escarpment, overlooking Burlington. The pond and the surrounding natural area were a conservation dream for Paul A. Fisher. This "big pond" and several others were designed to provide the necessary irrigation for fruit-tree orchards below the escarpment. The Bruce Trail has passed through this property for many years, thanks to the generous permission of the landowners. In 2018, the Fisher's Pond Side Trail officially became part of the Bruce Trail Conservancy.

Fisher's Pond Stile

Fisher's Pond

Distance
7 km

Terrain
Hilly, rocky, steep sections, creek-bed crossings, bridge, boardwalks, fields

Location and Parking
Near 3400 Guelph Line, Burlington

The Bruce Trail crosses Guelph Line about 1.5 km north of Dundas Street.

On the west side near open fields, look for a split-rail fence and ladder stile. 43.3880805°N-79.8536682°W

Summary of Hike
This is part loop, part out-and-back hike using Bruce Trail white blazes and side trail blue blazes.

1. At the stile entry, follow the path to the tree line and into the woods. Continue to follow the white blazes up the escarpment.

2. At the intersection of blue and white blazes at the top, turn left following the white blazes alongside the field. Before the trail bends right, step off the trail to view the lookout on the left, with views of Lake Ontario and Burlington.

3. Step back to the white blazes and follow them straight ahead. Continue following white blazes to the intersection with the Fisher's Pond Side Trail.

4. At the Fisher's Pond Side Trail, keep right to follow the blue blazes around the pond, returning to the intersection of blue and white blazes at the top edge of the escarpment.

5. At the intersection of blue and white blazes, turn left to follow the white blazes back to Guelph Line.

Route Map

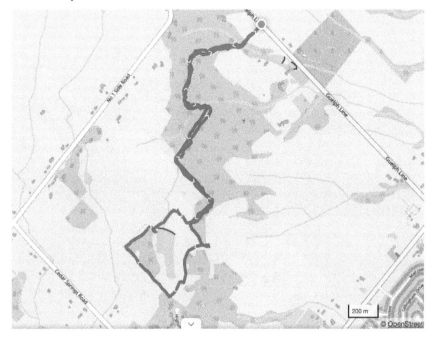

Features and Information

On this hike, Grindstone Creek transforms from shallow and gentle flows to the rocky Cascading Falls to the Great Falls at Smokey Hollow in Waterdown. The creek features a possible beaver habitat. The trail to the falls is hilly and increasingly rugged. The route is one of the longest and most challenging in this book and can be split as two separate hikes. For just the falls portion, skip steps 5 through 8, bypassing the bridge on the return (5 km route). To explore the loop only, skip steps 3 and 4 (7 km route).

Grindstone Creek

Trout Lily

Distance
9 km

Terrain
Mainly hilly, rocky, steep sections, uneven footing, bridge, boardwalks. Usually muddy and slippery when wet or icy.

Location and Parking
1451 Hidden Valley Rd, Burlington, L7R 3X5

Parking at the dead end of Hidden Valley Rd
43.3110874°N, 79.8768679° W

Summary of Hike
This is an out-and-back route to Smokey Hollow Falls, and a loop across the creek, using the Bruce Trail white blazes and many unmarked trails.

1. From the end of the road, walk along the creek to the first steep hill. Climb the hill and down to the trail that will narrow on a steep side slope. Go over, under, or around fallen trees.

2. Continue the trail. On the third steep climb, and at a split in the trail, keep left around a tree and descend to the creek.

3. At the bridge, stay to the right of the creek and continue by following the white blazes to the base of the falls. This is the turnaround point.

   Option: Climb the stairs to top of falls.

4. Retrace the route to the bridge, following the white blazes.

5. At the bridge, cross over and continue following the white blazes along and then above the creek (beaver habitat may be visible below on the right), then descend again.

6. At the lowest point nearer the creek (when the white blazes bend sharply right), turn left on the unmarked trail with a boardwalk, and continue straight ahead on this ascending trail (avoid side trails).

7. At the three-point intersection near the top, turn right on a narrow path then turn right at the T-intersection. Continue along the pastures (fencing); the trail follows close to the top edge of the valley and gradually into the woods.

8. At the intersection with white blazes on a post, turn right and continue with the white blazes to return to the bridge. Cross over and turn right.

9. Retrace the route on the unmarked trail and continue to parking area.

Route Map

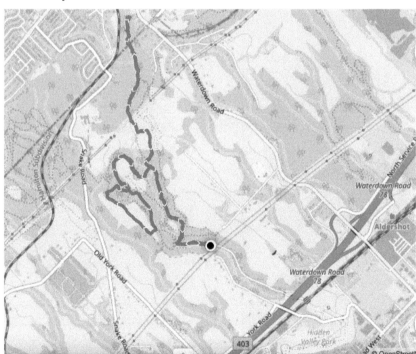

Features and Information

This hike includes interesting ruins, and meanders along Bronte Creek, edged with willow trees. The ruins are of a stone homestead from a nearby mill that were built by land surveyor James Cleaver in the 1800s. The stone wall shown in the photo collapsed in 2021 (other walls remain). The hike turnaround point at the mill site is near the village of Lowville. Some hikers like to venture a little further for lunch at the Lowville Bistro before returning to the trail to complete the hike.

Boardwalk

The Former Ruins

Distance
8 km

Terrain

Hilly, steep sections, flat sections, easy and uneven footing, bridges, boardwalks

Location and Parking
South end of Twiss Road at 8 Side Road, near the village of Kilbride (north Burlington)

Roadside parking
43.42942°N, 79.92721°W

Summary of Hike
Mainly using the Bruce Trail white blazes and marked side trail blue blazes, this is a loop hike with an out-and-back section reaching the village of Lowville on Guelph Line.

1. At the trailhead entrance on 8 Side Road, follow the white blazes as they continue into the valley, across a boardwalk, over the long bridge, and straight ahead away from the creek (ignore side trails).

2. At the sign for River and Ruin Side Trail, turn left following the blue blazes down towards the creek (ignore side trails).

3. At the sign for Squire Cleaver Side Trail, turn sharply left on the unmarked trail into the trees (do not turn onto Squire Cleaver Trail). This short path leads to the ruins.

4. Turn back from the ruins to return to the River and Ruin Side Trail and continue following the blue blazes to the creek.

5. At the gate, walk through the stile on the unmarked trail along the creek and continue to a private road. Turn left to the concrete bridge to view the falls and former mill site. This is the turnaround point for this section.

6. From the bridge, retrace the route on the unmarked trail as far as the gate. After the stile, keep right on the River and Ruin Side Trail, following the blue blazes along the creek. **Note:** there is signage to re-route to a parallel trail away from the creek when water levels are high in the spring (High Water Side Trail).

7. Continue following the blue blazes along the creek, crossing stiles and a small bridge, and keep right until meeting the white blazes.

8. At the white and blue blaze intersection turn right across the bridge; continue to follow the white blazes to retrace the route to Twiss Road and 8 Side Road.

Route Map

Features and Information

This hike is consistently hilly and a good workout, one of the most challenging of our hikes. It is best suited to the drier conditions in late spring through early fall, and is often too muddy and slippery when wet or icy. The first half of the route passes through Clappison Woods Conservation Area. The high point near the pond was a former quarry. There is a small stone ruin at the turnaround point.

Crossing the Creek and Bridge

The Ruins

Distance
6 km

Terrain.
Very rugged, rocky, hilly, uneven footing, boardwalk, bridges, stairs, rail-line crossing

Location and Parking
Near 1800 Snake Rd, Burlington, L7P 4Y3

Roadside parking near the hydro tower lines about 0.8 km north of Old York Road.
43.31744° N, 79.89237° W

Summary of Hike
This is an out-and-back hike using the Bruce Trail white blazes, starting from the west side of Snake Road.

1. From the Bruce Trail sign near the road, start the route at the stairs and follow the white blazes through the woods, avoiding unmarked side trails.

2. At the top, after passing the pond and descending the stairs, the trail turns right. Continue following the blazes until reaching the ruins. This is the turnaround point.

   Option: Go through the tunnel to see the graffiti and the panoramic view of Hamilton on the other side of the highway.

3. To finish the hike, turn back and retrace the route, following the white blazes to Snake Road. Stay on the marked trail.

Route Map

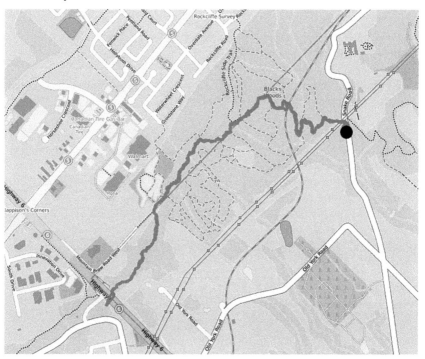

Features and Information

This hike includes sections of Crawford Lake and Rattlesnake Point Conservation Areas and is a good hike for any season. It is highlighted by escarpment lookouts and spring wildflowers. The valley at the south end of the hike was a former buffalo compound managed by the Conservation Area in the late 1960s. The buffalo were moved to the Mountsberg Area in the 1990s before the program ended.

Buffalo Chute

Rock Crevices

Distance
7 km

Terrain
Rocky and steep sections, flat sections, creeks, boardwalks, mainly good footing

Location and Parking
The south end of Canyon Road, Milton

Paved parking area at the dead end, and roadside parking.
43.483540,-79.951892

Summary of Hike
This is a loop hike and includes a short out-and-back section to Buffalo Crag Lookout, using the Bruce Trail white blazes, side trail blue blazes, and unmarked trails.

1. An unmarked trail starts immediately from the parking area. After about 400m, turn left on a small, unmarked trail; this parallels the first trail for a few hundred metres and is used to avoid several wet areas.

2. At the large multi-trail intersection, turn left on the Jack Leech-Porter Side Trail. Follow the blue blazes up and out of the canyon. Avoid unmarked side trails.

3. At the top, the trail bends right. At post RP10, stay straight ahead following the white blazes towards Rattlesnake Point.

4. At the three-point intersection at post RP09, stay straight ahead and follow the blue blazes on Rattlesnake Point Side Trail.

5. When the side trail splits (both sides marked with blue blazes), turn right and follow through a rugged section of rock formations and crevices to Buffalo Crag Lookout. This is the turnaround point.

6. Turn back, following the blue blazes. Turn left at the split and return to the three-point intersection.

7. At post RP09, turn left to follow the white blazes down the canyon.

8. At the T-intersection at the bottom, turn left on the unmarked trail into a fenced area. Turn right to see the remnants of the buffalo compound (large chute and staging area). Return to the main trail, turn left, and follow the white blazes over the creek to the access road.

9. At the access road, turn right and continue towards Canyon Road.

10. At the large multi-trail intersection (Jack Leech-Porter Side Trail is on the right), stay straight ahead and continue along the unmarked trail.

11. The split for the parallel trail section may not be obvious (optional route turns left); the return route stays straight ahead.

12. At the T-intersection, turn right for the final 400m to the parking area.

Route Map

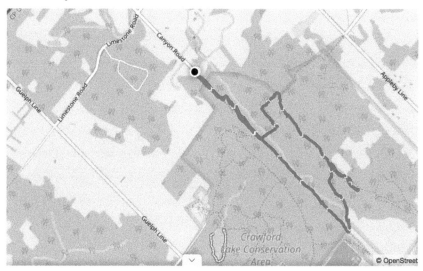

Features and Information

The Halton Regional Forests are 14 separate tracts totalling 703 hectares, and include wooded areas, wetlands, and meadows. These tracts provide rich and varied wildlife habitats and are home to several rare species. The areas are publicly accessible, with many trail loops to explore via hikes or bikes. At Hilton Falls, the stone structures are ruins of 19th century sawmills. The creek and dam powered a massive 40-foot-diameter water wheel. Fires destroyed the mills, and the site was abandoned in 1967.

Hilton Falls

Marsh Marigolds in Spring

Distance
6 km

Terrain
Mainly narrow bike trails, rocky, uneven footing, boardwalks, bridges, stairs

Location and Parking
10 Side Road and Fourth Line
Nassagaweya, Milton

Roadside parking at the corner intersection
43.51574° N, 79.99749° W

Summary of Hike
This is a loop hike with an out-and-back section to Hilton Falls. The trails are named; however, not all have signs posted.

1. The route begins at the sign for Mahon Tract and Turner Tract, starting down the gravel access road. After a short distance, turn left on the gravel road and over a raised boardwalk.

2. Continue a quick section of splits, keeping right at each, following these landmarks: cross the log boardwalk, step over a log, step through the cut of a large fallen tree, and continue.

3. At the intersection at post HF15, keep right on Five Bridges.

4. At the T-intersection, turn left (parallel to the creek), and a quick left at the next split (Five Bridges sign after the split).

5. At post HF16, turn right on Hiltons Hwy, and at post HF21 turn left to The Falls.

6. As the sound of the falls becomes very close, step off the trail on the right for a quick partial view of the falls. Step back to the trail to continue the route to the bridge that crosses the creek above the falls.

7. From the bridge, turn right (stay left of the blue blazes), then keep right, following the signs to the falls. The metal stairs descend to the lookout.

   This is the turnaround point.

8. Continue the return portion from the falls:
   - Circle back to the trail and at post HF05 turn left to the bridge. Cross over and continue the other side.
   - At the intersection at post HF21 turn right, and at post HF16 turn left.

9. To finish the loop portion of the hike, keep left at the next intersection, crossing a bridge with a railing. After the bridge the trail splits; take either side to meet the cross trail, turn right, and continue.

10. On the boardwalk that splits, keep right and continue. The trail meets the gravel access road; keep straight ahead for the short walk to the parking area.

Route Map

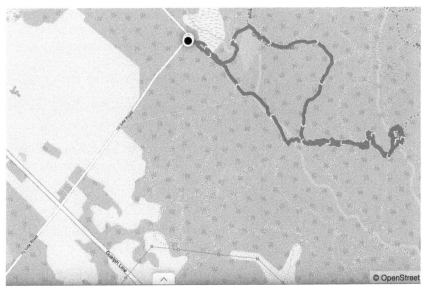

Features and Information

Cedar and pine forest, and a small pond attracting songbirds and heron are on the west route. Rock caves and a rock wall, and many spring wildflowers, are on the east route. The east route has an access road running parallel to the Bruce Trail. For part of the route they overlap, providing an easy walking section. This area is called the Calcium Pits, named from small ponds lined with marl. The marl was used in whitewash and tiles, and for insecticide before DDT became popular.

Twiss West: The Pond

Twiss East: The Wall

Distance
6 km and 4 km (two routes)

Terrain
West route: some rocky sections, some hills, uneven footing.

East route: mainly flat, rocky, uneven footing, two short steep sections.

Location and Parking
Near 7420 Twiss Road, Milton

The Bruce Trail crosses Twiss Road at the bottom of a steep S-curve, about 1.8 km north of Derry Road.

Roadside parking on both sides of the road. Use caution due to the steep, blind curves.
43.448010 N, 79.953700 W

Summary of Hike
These are out-and-back hikes on the Bruce Trail using white blazes, about 1.5 hours duration per route.

WEST: Twiss Road to Derry Road and Back
1. The trailhead is south of the parallel parking area on the west side.

2. Follow the white blazes and continue until reaching Derry Road. Return on the same route, stay on marked trail.

Option to explore the pond:

Early into the hike, at the marked left turn, keep right on the small, unmarked trail to the pond (use caution close to the pond due to poor footing). Return to the marked trail to continue the hike.

EAST: Twiss Road to Guelph Line and Back

1. The trailhead is north of the parking area on the east side.

2. Follow the white blazes (including over the rock wall) and continue until reaching Guelph Line. Return on the same route, stay on the marked trail.

Route Maps

West Route

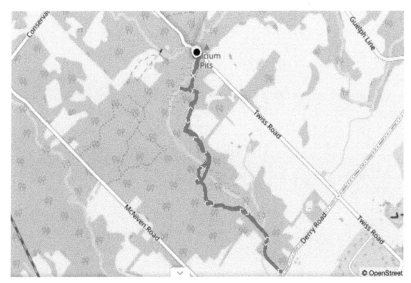

East Route

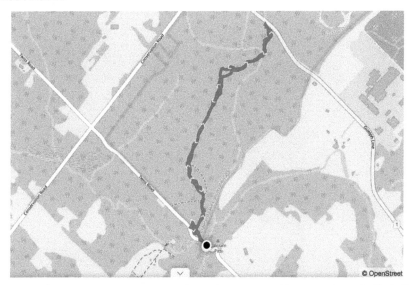

Features and Information

This hike has panoramic views of the valley and up-close experiences with Borer's Falls. There is also a ruin of a homestead fence at the top of the escarpment. Borer's Falls, also known as Rock Chapel Falls, is a 15-metre-high ribbon-style falls with more than 100 years of history. The falls originally powered the Rock Chapel Village sawmill, which was owned by the Borer family. The hike follows the RBG Escarpment Trail, arriving at the old Sugar Shack. Annually, until the late 1970s, it was used to make maple syrup and host pancake breakfasts in the spring.

Borer's Falls

View of the Bridge

Distance
7 km

Terrain
Some very steep hills, rocky, narrow paths, stairs, short roadside walk

Location and Parking
Borer's Falls Dog Park
491 York Road, Dundas, L9H 5Z9

Summary of Hike
This is an out-and-back hike using a Bruce Trail side trail and the Bruce Trail, as well as the RBG Escarpment Trail.

1. From the parking lot, follow the blue blazes to the Ray Lowes Side Trail.

2. Follow the blue blazes through the forest, avoiding side trails until meeting the white blazes. Follow the white blazes left.

3. Shortly after the stairs, there is a narrow, unmarked path on the right that leads to a stone-fence ruin. Step off the Bruce Trail to see the ruin, then return to the trail and follow the white blazes and Escarpment Trail signs.

4. Continue to a stone wall and clearing on the left, where there is a safe place to view the falls.

5. Continue following the white blazes over the bridge and along the road. Just after crossing the Rock Chapel parking lot, there is a curved path that leads to another lookout. Follow the path back to the Escarpment Trail, turning left to continue.

6. Continue the trail to the Sugar Shack and pavilion. There is a lookout platform just in front of the pavilion. This is the turnaround point.

7. To finish the hike, retrace the route, following the white blazes to the intersection of the white and blue blazes. Turn right to follow the blue blazes back to the parking lot.

Route Map

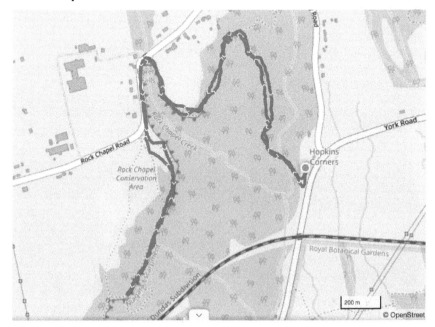

Features and Information

This hike features a dam, Darnley Waterfall, and mill ruins. The mill was part of the Crooks' Hollow village in 1813.

Christie Lake Dam was built in 1970 to form a reservoir to control flooding from Spencer's Gorge and the many waterfalls in the area. Christie Lake Conservation Area offers picnicking, hiking, biking, swimming, kayaking and disc golf.

Christie Lake

The Dam Entrance

Distance
8 km

Terrain
Dirt trails, grassy fields, some low hills, road crossings, dam crossing, pavement

Location and Parking
756 Crooks' Hollow Road, Dundas, L9H 5EZ

Parking lot on Crooks' Hollow Road
Membership or parking payment required
43.27683^0 N, 80.00100^0 W

Summary of Hike
This is a loop hike around the lake after entering the conservation area. Yellow arrows guide the hiker but are infrequently spaced.

1. Facing Crooks' Hollow Road, find a path on the left marked with a yellow arrow. Follow the yellow arrows, crossing over Crooks' Hollow and Cramer Road to the Christie Lake entrance.

2. Continue to the dam and turn left across it.

    Option: Turn left on the dirt road to the waterfall lookout; return to the dam exit.

3. After crossing the dam, turn right and follow yellow arrows along the shoreline. Continue for about 2 km, turning right at trail splits. **Do not take the by-pass trail. Follow yellow arrows.**

4. At the multi-trail intersection, keep right and follow yellow arrows to

Wedlen Trail, then follow yellow arrows along shoreline to a T-intersection with a road. Turn right onto the road.

5. At the road intersection, turn right and cross over the narrow end of the lake. Turn right again past the boat launch area. Walk on the grass, following the shoreline with the lake on right, passing the swimming area to a black fence.

6. At the black fence, turn left and follow the fence line to an opening. Turn right, cross over a small bridge, turn right and cross towards the lake. At the signpost with yellow arrows, turn left onto a grassy path. Follow the yellow arrows along the lake to the road, parking lot, and chain-link fence.

7. Follow the chain-link fence past Marina Pavilion, turning slightly left, and continue along the sidewalk to the McCoy Pavilion. Walk around the pavilion and cross the field to a path on the opposite side. Continue to follow the yellow arrows up the hill, into the woods through a rail fence, and past a disc golf station. Keep left to stay on the path into the woods.

8. The trail returns to the dam. Follow the yellow arrows left, retrace the route back to the Christie Lake entrance, across Cramer and Crooks' Hollow Road, turning left at the trail intersection and continuing through the woods back to the parking lot.

Route Map

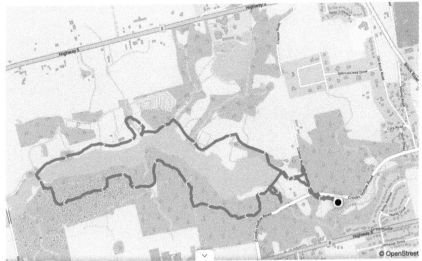

Features and Information

Christie Lake is a reservoir lake where swimming, kayaking, disc golf, and picnicking are enjoyed throughout the summer. There is also a biking track. The Christie Lake Dam, built in the 1970s, harnesses the water from Spencer's Gorge and the many waterfalls in the area. Close to the dam is the tiered Darnley Waterfall and the ruins of the profitable mill that contributed to the industry of Crooks' Hollow in the 1860s.

The Dam

Christie Lake

Distance
8.5 km

Terrain
Dirt trails, grassy fields, some low hills, road crossings, dam crossing, pavement

Location and Parking
405 Middletown Rd, Dundas, L9H 5E2

White-Tailed Deer Access Trail Parking About 0.8 km south of Hwy 5, look for the gravel lane on the west side (through trees).

Membership or parking payment required
43.27811^0 N, 80.03614^0 W

Summary of Hike
Once the lake has been accessed, this is a loop around Christie Lake using yellow arrows that are infrequently spaced.

1. Enter the path to the left of the parking pay station. This leads to Middletown Road. At the intersection, turn left, cross the road, and around the gate to walk up the road.

2. At the intersection, turn right then left to a path that is close to the lake (picnic tables are straight ahead). Follow the yellow arrows.

3. Walk on the grass, following the shoreline with the lake on right, passing the swimming area to a black fence.

4. At the black fence, turn left and follow the fence line to an opening. Turn right, cross over a small bridge, turn right and cross towards the lake. At the signpost with yellow arrows, turn left onto a grassy path. Follow the yellow arrows along the lake to the road, parking lot, and chain-link fence.

5. Follow the chain-link fence past Marina Pavilion, turning slightly left, and continue along the sidewalk to the McCoy Pavilion. Walk around the pavilion and cross the field to a path on the opposite side. Continue to follow the yellow arrows up the hill, into the woods through a rail fence, and past a disc golf station. Keep left to stay on the path into the woods.

6. At the intersection near the woods, turn right to cross the dam.

    Option: Turn left on the dirt road to the waterfall lookout; return to the dam exit.

7. After crossing the dam, follow the yellow arrows to hike the opposite side of the lake for 2 km, turning right at trail splits. **Do not take the by-pass trail. Follow yellow arrows.**

8. At the multi-trail intersection, keep right and follow yellow arrows to Wedlen Trail, then follow yellow arrows along shoreline to a T-intersection with a road. Turn right onto the road.

9. Continue to green gates. Just after the green gates, turn left onto the road that leads to Middletown Road. Turn right at Middletown Road and cross the road to parking lot on left.

Route Map

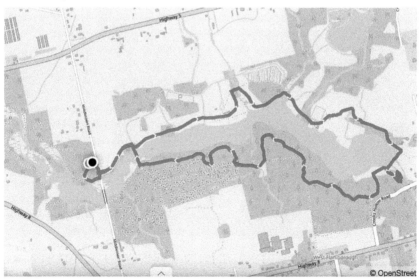

© OpenStreet

Features and Information

Dundas Peak, in the Spencer Gorge Conservation Area, is one of the most popular spots in Hamilton, and offers amazing views of the area. Tew Falls is also part of this hike. It is 41 metres high, almost as high as Niagara Falls. The platforms allow good views of the falls. Part of the side trail uses the old tracks from the Great Western Railway (1853). Due to erosion, and following a train wreck in the 1930s, the train track was abandoned.

Stone Stairs to the Peak

Tew Falls

Distance
7 km

Terrain
Some steep inclines, good footing, dirt paths, stone and wood stairs, short residential walk

Location and Parking
Dundas Driving Park
71 Cross Street, Dundas, L9H 2R7

Park near the houses in the Driving Park.

Summary of Hike
This is an out-and-back hike with a short residential walk to the Bruce Trail white blazes, then using side trail blue blazes.

1. Take the paved path beside house #22 in the park and walk along Cayley Street to Sydenham Road. Cross Sydenham and turn right to the white blazes behind the guardrail.

2. Follow the white blazes across a small bridge. Turn left when the white blazes turn right and follow the unmarked trail up the wooden stairs.

3. At the top of the wood stairs, turn left, cross a bridge, turn right and under an underpass, then left to the back of a stone wall and look for blue blazes to continue.

4. Follow the blue blazes up sets of stairs and along the old railway path, avoiding side trails.

5. At the top of the long flight of stone stairs, turn left and continue following the trail to the black

fence, turning left to the Dundas Peak viewing platform. Turn back to the trail and turn left to continue.

6. At the end of a wood rail fence is the first viewing platform for Tew Falls; although, due to foliage, it is difficult to see.

7. Continue the trail across a bridge that crosses a gap. Shortly after this is the second viewing platform on the left and stairs straight ahead that lead to the third viewing platform. This is the turnaround point.

8. Retrace the route up the stairs, following blue blazes to the bridge that crosses the gap. At the intersection at the gap, turn left onto the Glen Ferguson Side Trail. Signage can be seen once on the trail.

9. Follow the blue blazes for 1.8 km to the end. Turn left onto the original side trail and retrace the route back to the white blazes.

10. Turn right to follow the white blazes, walking behind the guardrail. After the guardrail, cross Sydenham Road and walk downhill to Cayley Street. Turn left onto Cayley and continue to the Dundas Driving Park.

Route Map

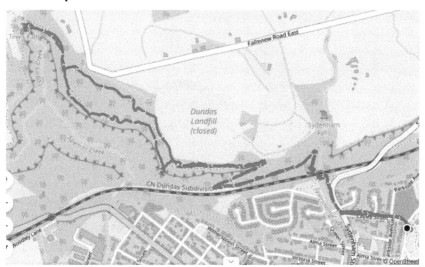

Features and Information

The McCormack is one of the seven trails that are part of the Dundas Valley. Some of this trail overlaps with the Bruce Trail, providing a varied terrain. It has a Carolinian Forest, meadows, a woodland pond, and a local horse farm. The pond is a salamander sanctuary. Stop at the pond to see and hear bullfrogs, herons, or turtles. This part of the valley is also home to many deer, foxes, and rabbits.

The Pond

Horse Farm

Distance
7 km

Terrain
Very hilly, some steep hills, narrow dirt paths, wide grassy trails, good footing

Location and Parking
Davidson Boulevard Access Trail
122 Newcombe Road, Dundas, L9H 0A6

Street parking, look for the stone pillars next to Valleyside Lane.

Summary of Hike
This is a loop hike using Bruce Trail white blazes, the McCormack Trail of the Dundas Valley, and local unmarked bicycle paths.

1. Enter the trail at the stone pillars. At the top of the hill, turn left and follow the white blazes.

2. At the end of a long boardwalk, just before the intersection with McCormack Trail, turn right onto a small, unmarked trail that leads into an evergreen forest. Avoid any side trails. Continue following this narrow path.

3. At the hill, keep right at the split and continue until the path ends at a T-intersection.

4. At the intersection, turn left and continue for approximately 300 metres to another unmarked trail on the right. Turn right, go under the slanted tree, follow the path

along the top edge of a ravine. Continue along this path until it comes to a small hill.

5. At the hill, turn left onto an unmarked path that crosses a lightly wooded area. (**Note:** in the fall this path is difficult to see due to falling leaves.) Cross the area to the opposite side, going up to a small, narrow path.

6. At the narrow path, turn right. Follow it as it dips and turns left.

7. At the T-intersection, turn left, follow the path to McCormack Trail and turn left. Continue to a multi-trail intersection where the white blazes and McCormack cross. Continue straight ahead, following the McCormack Trail to the top of the lookout hill. There are benches at the top.

8. Go down the other side of the lookout hill. At the first wide path at the bottom of the hill, turn right. Continue to the next intersection.

9. At the intersection with white blazes, turn left and follow the blazes down the hill. Look for a pond on the right. Continue to the bottom of the hill to the horse farm on left. This is the turnaround point.

10. To return, follow the white blazes straight ahead to the multi-trail intersection (avoid side trails). Continue straight onto the boardwalk and follow the white blazes back to the access trail intersection, turn right onto the access trail, and continue to the road and parking.

Route Map

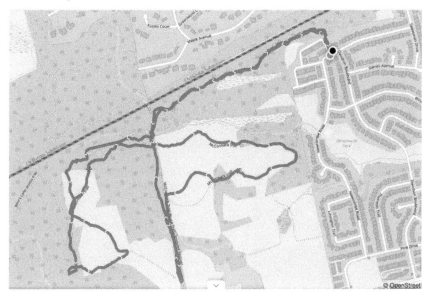

Features and Information

Griffin House:

Griffin House was built in 1857 by one of the first black settlers in the area.

The Hermitage Ruins:

The Hermitage and Gatehouse Museum is maintained by the Hamilton Conservation Authority. Built prior to 1853, the Hermitage had several owners before being purchased by George Browne Leith and his wife. The area reminded them of Scotland. After Mrs. Leith's death, the property was purchased by the youngest daughter. She lived in the house until it was destroyed by fire in 1934. The ruins are said to be haunted and are often used for spooky evening hikes.

Griffin House

The Hermitage Ruins

Distance
7 km

Terrain
Wide paths, easy footing, some hilly sections

Location and Parking
Ancaster Lions Outdoor Pool
263 Jerseyville Rd West, Ancaster, L9G 2B8

Additional parking across the road at the park.

Summary of Hike
This is an out-and-back hike. The trails are named; however, not all have signs posted.

1. The Spring Valley Trail starts down the left side of the pool building and follows along the creek. At the Spring Valley signpost, turn right over the bridge and left to follow on the other side of the creek.

2. At the intersection, keep right to go uphill (Hilltop Trail). At the next intersection and signposts, stay straight on Headwaters Trail.

3. At the multi-trail intersection (large information sign), turn right to continue along Headwaters Trail.

4. After the bridge (at the wooden bench), keep left on Headwaters and continue, crossing Mineral Springs Road. Watch for the sign for Griffin House.

5. At the sign for Griffin House, turn left on the side trail, explore the

site, and return to the main route, turning left on Headwaters Trail. Continue and cross over Sulphur Springs Road and follow signs for Hermitage.

6. At the next intersection, turn left on the Bruce Trail (white blazes) to reach the access road, and turn right to explore the Hermitage site. This is the turnaround point.

7. To finish the hike, return to the access road and retrace the route:

   i. At the Bruce Trail turn left with the white blazes.
   ii. At Headwaters Trail, turn right and continue, crossing both roads.
   iii. At the intersection (wooden bench), keep right over the bridge.
   iv. At the large information sign, turn left and keep left on Headwaters Trail.
   v. At the split, keep right on Headwaters Trail.
   vi. At the intersection, stay straight ahead on Hilltop Trail, and at the bottom keep left along the creek.
   vii. Turn right over the bridge and left to continue along the creek (Spring Valley Trail) for the last stretch to the parking lot.

Route Map

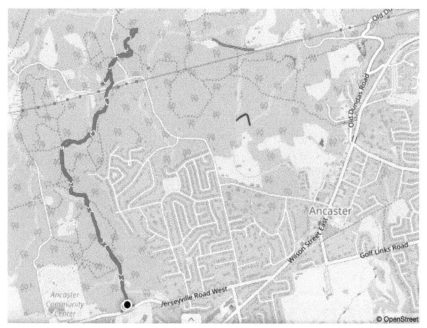

Features and Information

This hike features three beautiful waterfalls.

Canterbury Falls, within the Dundas Valley, is a 9-metre ribbon waterfall, which can freeze in winter. The area is lush with trees and foliage.

Sherman Falls, also known as Angel Falls or Fairy Falls, is a 17-metre curtain waterfall. It is named after the Sherman family, who once owned the property and were important community members.

Tiffany Falls is a 21-metre ribbon waterfall named after Dr. Oliver Tiffany, who was the first doctor in the area in the 1860s.

Canterbury Falls

Sherman Falls

THREE WATERFALLS HIKE

Distance
7 km

Terrain
Mix of rocky, hilly, and flat trails

Location and Parking
Ancaster Mill Chapel, Upper Parking
490 Old Dundas Road, Ancaster

Use the top level of the upper parking lot across the road from the chapel.

Summary of Hike
This is an out-and-back hike starting in the Dundas Valley, mostly using Bruce Trail white blazes and side trail blue blazes.

1. Walking towards the parking lot entrance, look on the left for a short path (an opening in the bushes) that leads to the Heritage Trail. Turn left.

2. Continue until the next trail intersection at posts on the right.

3. At the posts marking Canterbury Falls Trail, turn right. It is marked as a blue side trail (if the donation collection box is reached, then the turn was missed). Continue until reaching Canterbury Falls.

4. At Canterbury Falls, turn right to follow white blazes and continue until reaching Sherman Falls. Turn right on the path on the right side of the creek to get closer to the falls.

5. Turn back to the intersection of blue and white blazes at the road.

6. Turn right to follow white blazes across the road at the corner of Old Dundas and Old Ancaster Road and follow white blazes into the woods.

7. Continue to follow white blazes to an intersection where white blazes meet blue blazes. Turn right onto the Tiffany Falls blue side trail and follow it across the road, the parking lot, and along the creek to Tiffany Falls. Take care crossing Wilson Street. This is the turnaround point.

8. To return, retrace the route, following blue blazes back across the road and down the stairs. Turn left to follow the white blazes.

9. Continue to follow the white blazes across the intersection of Old Dundas and Old Ancaster Road, passing Sherman Falls, and keeping right to go up the hill away from the falls. Continue to Canterbury Falls.

10. At Canterbury Falls, turn left onto Canterbury Falls blue side trail, and then left again onto Heritage Trail at the intersection. Follow Heritage Trail back to parking.

Route Map

Features and Information

This hike is along Spencer Creek. Children enjoy the hike since it is easy to navigate and is mainly flat. There is a mix of forest, wetlands, and some historical artifacts along the route. The 22-metre-high curtain waterfalls and 78 acres of the surrounding land were purchased by Joseph Webster after his family arrived from England in 1820. Their gravestones are in the park. Once used to generate electricity and power mills, the area was repurposed as a park in 1933. It is often used in movies.

Webster Falls

Cobblestone Bridge

Distance
6 km

Terrain
Mainly flat, dirt paths, bridges, short roadside walk

Location and Parking
756 Crooks' Hollow Road, Dundas, L9H 5EZ

Parking lot on Crooks' Hollow Road
Membership or parking payment required
43.27683° N, 80.00100° W

Summary of Hike
This is an out-and-back hike with a loop at the turnaround point. Spencer Adventure signs and orange arrows are posted on the trail. The pedestrian entrance to Webster Falls is at the first gatehouse/fence on Fallsview Rd. The gate may be closed but not locked. **Note:** refer to website for seasonal reservations.

1. At the large information sign located in the parking lot, take the path on the right leading towards the creek. At the bottom of the stone steps, turn left to follow the gorge. At the split, continue close to the creek, bypassing the brown bridge.

2. Continue the trail over multiple boardwalks, under Brock Road, and over Spencer Creek, following signs.

3. At the old stone wall, turn right and then left to go up and around it. At the bridge, turn left and cross.

4. At the end of the bridge, turn right onto a residential road (Fallsview Rd) and walk to an iron fence and small gatehouse on the right. Go through gate and follow the path downhill, crossing a park towards the first bridge.

5. Cross the bridge, climb the stairs, turn left, and walk towards an opening to the falls viewing area.

6. Exiting the viewing area, turn right at the cobblestone bridge. Turn right again to follow the fence line to view the falls on the other side. Continue to follow the path into a wooded area.

7. At the first dirt path in the wooded area, turn left. Continue to follow this path. At the split, keep right to the stairs to the tiny Webster family cemetery.

8. After the cemetery, continue straight ahead across the parking lot. At the sidewalk, turn left and then right, following the black fence line near the falls. Turn right at the intersection to continue past the park to the gatehouse. This completes the turnaround loop.

9. Retrace the route to return; turn left out of the gate and left to cross the bridge (just after Short Road sign). Turn right onto the trail and right around the stone wall to the creek. At the creek, turn left on the trail to continue the route along the creek to parking.

Route Map

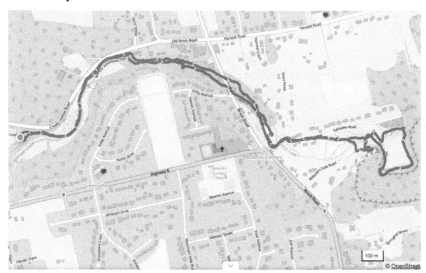

Features and Information

The beginning of this hike visits Chedoke Falls, a 15.5-metre urban ribbon waterfall, almost hidden off the Bruce Trail. The trail meanders above the Chedoke golf course. The area is thickly wooded and rocky. The photo shows the typical rock face of the escarpment. After a short urban section this hike returns to the Chedoke Radial Trail, a 9.5 km popular multi-use trail.

There are five sets of city-built escarpment stairs in Hamilton, ranging in length from 227 to 387 stairs. They are well-used for exercise, commuting to and from work, and accessing trails. Some sets are wider and divided by a handrail, and some have a bicycle trough.

The Bruce Trail

Spring in the Forest

Distance
6 km

Terrain
Rocky, tree roots, some steep inclines, fields, sidewalks, stairs, road crossing

Location and Parking
Chedoke Golf Club, Clubhouse parking
Beddoe Drive, Hamilton
43.24608°N, 79.90796°W

Summary of Hike
This is a loop hike using the Chedoke and Dundurn Stairs, Bruce Trail white blazes, and the Chedoke Radial Trail.

1. At the stairs in the parking lot, climb approximately halfway. Exit the stairs at the white blazes.

2. Follow the white blazes to the end of a wood railing. Pause to look sharply to the right to view Chedoke Falls. Continue left to the bottom of the hill.

3. At the intersection with the Radial Trail, turn right and then right again at the white blazes. Continue following the white blazes to Beckett Drive, avoiding side trails.

4. At Beckett Drive, cross the road carefully and continue the trail on the other side.

5. Near the top of a hill (before the overpass), turn right on the cement stairs and move through the gate to the field.

6. Cross the field diagonally, staying left of the radio tower ahead. On the left side of the tower, enter an unmarked path through a metal

gate to a small wooded area. Turn left to cross the area, keeping right to the opposite corner.

7. At the split, keep right and continue the path along the fence line on the left, with cliff edge on the right.

8. At the end of the clifftop, turn left through an opening in the fence to a field. Continue across the field diagonally, keeping right to the sidewalk.

9. At the sidewalk, turn right onto Fennel Avenue, continue to Garth Street, cross, turn right and continue to Beckett Road sign. Turn left to take the Dundurn stairs all the way down to the Radial Trail.

10. At the intersection with the Radial Trail, turn left and walk back to the Chedoke parking lot.

Route Map

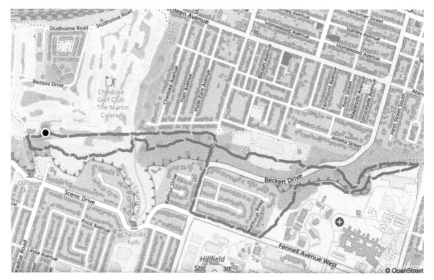

Features and Information

The Chedoke Radial Trail is a 2.7-kilometre section of the Bruce Trail, designed to be a pedestrian and bicycle pathway. It is built on what was once the Brantford and Hamilton Electric Railway. There are several waterfalls on this hike. Many of them are seasonal or culvert falls of various sizes. Princess Falls drops about 7 metres, flows under the trail, and plunges over 30 metres to Hwy 403. This waterfall was altered to build the highway, by cutting into the escarpment. The tunnel at the beginning of the hike was used to pass under a ski hill, when Chedoke was a ski resort.

The Radial Trail

Upper Princess Falls

Distance
9 km

Terrain
Wide and narrow paths, rocky, tree roots, hilly, some steep inclines

Location and Parking
Chedoke Golf Club, Clubhouse parking Beddoe Drive, Hamilton 43.24608°N, 79.90796°W

Summary of Hike
This hike has three parts. It begins by following the Bruce Trail white blazes, then diverges to local hiking paths, looping back to Radial Trail side trail blue blazes and then Bruce Trail white blazes.

1. Start this hike at the Radial Trail and white blazes in the parking lot (near the clubhouse). Continue following the Radial Trail and white blazes over bridges, through a tunnel, and past waterfalls.

2. At the intersection of blue and white blazes under the hydro lines, follow the white blazes to the right through the woods. Following the white blazes, continue towards the fence line and into an open field area. Ignore side trails crossing the field.

3. At the split intersection before entering a wooded area, leave the white blazes and proceed straight ahead into the bush.

4. Follow this unmarked side trail through a lowland area. There are several trails, but always keep to

the right. The trail heads to a fence and along the edge of the escarpment beside Hwy 403, ending at the Radial Trail.

5. At the intersection with the Radial Trail, turn right. Just before reaching the bridge, turn left onto a narrow, unmarked path heading up. Step up a small hill, keeping right.

6. There are several intersections along this path—always keep right. The trail descends into a valley and then ascends to an intersection with an open field ahead. Turn left, going over or around a fallen tree to an open area, and continue towards some large rocks.

7. At the intersection just past the rocks, turn left onto a wider path leading to a steep hill. Turn right to descend the hill ending at the Radial Trail.

8. At the Radial Trail, turn right and continue, avoid side trails. At the intersection of blue and white blazes under the hydro lines, continue following the Radial Trail and white blazes to the parking lot.

Route Map

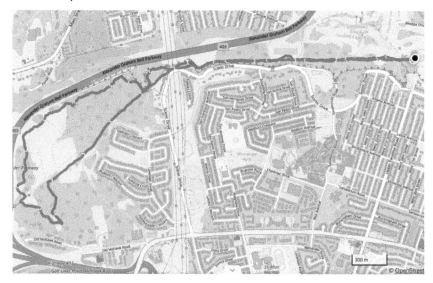

Features and Information

The RBG trails are easy to follow and great for the family. Explore further by viewing the collections or visiting the Interpretive Centre. A variety of outdoor spaces and activities will connect visitors to the wetlands, forest, and wildlife. The Anishinaabe Waadiziwin sanctuary opened in 2015 to acknowledge the importance of Indigenous peoples in the area. The plant uses described on the trail reflect traditional Anishinaabe knowledge and cultural beliefs.

Homestead Trail

View from the Shore

Distance
7 km

Terrain
Wide trails, easy footing, some steep sections, boardwalks, bridges

Location and Parking
Royal Botanical Gardens Arboretum
16 Old Guelph Rd, Hamilton, L0R 2H9

Membership or parking payment required.

Park near the kiosk and Interpretive Centre or in the circular lot next to the Arboretum.

Summary of Hike
This route is a clockwise loop and is usually less than two hours to complete.

RBG trails are named and signs are posted.

1. On the left side of the Interpretive Centre, the route begins on Anishinaabe Waadiziwin Trail leading down to the shoreline, across the floating bridge, and through the sanctuary.

2. Use the signs to continue in the direction of Marsh Walk.

3. At Bull's Point Trail, turn left for a short out-and-back walk to a raised lookout. Return to the signposts at the intersection and continue straight on Bull's Point Trail to Marsh Walk.

4. At Marsh Walk, turn left, descending to a boardwalk and raised lookout. Exiting the boardwalk, turn left to ascend Marsh Walk to the intersection.

5. At Bull's Point Trail, turn left and continue a longer section of the route.

6. At the three-point intersection, keep right on Homestead Trail.

7. At Gray Doe Trail (immediately after crossing through the hydro tract and towers, look right for the trail intersection, before the bridge with railing), turn right, continuing through ravines and descending to the water.

8. At the bottom of Grey Doe Trail, turn left over the bridge and left on Hickory Valley, ascending through the woods to the Arboretum.

9. Walk around or through the Arboretum and return to the parking lot.

Route Map

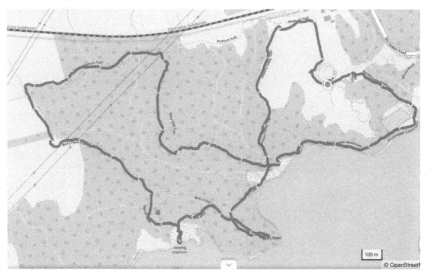

Features and Information

Established in 1927 for its significance as a migratory bird stopover, Cootes Paradise is RBG's largest and most diverse sanctuary. The area features a large river-mouth marsh, 16 creeks and 25 km of shoreline.

The Desjardins Canal, originally built for shipping, became a fishway that allows movement of native species and keeps invasive species out of the marsh. The water access at Princess Point is popular all year for activities such as paddling, ice skating, and hockey.

The Edge of the Marsh

Along the Trail

Distance
9 km

Terrain
Hilly, steep sections, boardwalks, stairs, urban park, some roadside sections

Location and Parking
Hamilton Aviary and RBG parking lot 85 Oak Knoll Drive, Hamilton, L8S 4C2 Membership or parking payment required

Summary of Hike
This is a longer loop hike with options to shorten or extend the route.

RBG trails are named, with signs posted.

1. Near the parking entrance, begin the hike on Caleb's Walk.

2. At Ravine Road Trail, turn left and continue until exiting the woods at the campus of McMaster University.

Optional Trail and Campus Loop (1 km)
At the campus edge behind Les Prince Hall, keep right to Chegwin Trail and keep right to the trail exit at Woodstock Hall. Keep left through campus to Les Prince Hall and return to Ravine Road Trail entrance.

3. At the edge of campus, re-enter Ravine Road Trail and retrace the route, bypassing Caleb's Walk. Continue along Ravine Road Trail.

Optional Side Trail (1.5 km)
At Sassafras Point Trail, turn left to complete the loop. Turn left on Ravine Road Trail to continue.

4. At Ginger Valley Trail (large stone pad and stairs on left), turn left, climb stairs, and continue through the forest. Near the park edge, keep left and follow the short boardwalk to stay in the forest.

5. The Ginger Valley Trail enters the west side of Churchill Park. At the park, turn left to walk around the north edge to the opposite corner. At the sign for Princess Point Trail, follow it behind the houses. At the T-intersection, turn left and continue.

6. In the field at the bottom of the hill, the next intersection is the other half of Princess Point Trail coming from Churchill Park. Keep right to continue Princess Point Trail towards the water. At the red Muskoka chairs, turn right, follow past the parking lot, and turn left to the loop around Princess Point and back to the red chairs.

7. From the red chairs, continue straight ahead (away from the water) and through the field to the intersection with Princess Point Trail. Turn right through the field then left to take Princess Point Trail back to the north end of Churchill Park.

8. At Churchill Park, turn right and follow the edge of the park all the way to the bottom/southwest end where the park reaches Marion Avenue North (trailhead for Ravine Road Trail on right).

9. At Marion Avenue, turn right and take the path through the grassy area past the aviary, and back to the RBG parking lot.

Route Map

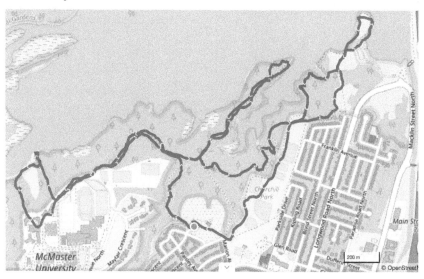

Features and Information

Often a dry waterfall, hikers can usually walk into the bowl of the waterfall. The Punchbowl is also known as Horseshoe Falls due to its distinctive shape. There are layers of stratified rock visible around the bowl. There are many stories as to why it is called the Devil's Punchbowl. One possibility is a reference to bootlegging that took place in the area in the 1920s. The monument and museum provide all the details of the decisive Battle of Stoney Creek, won here by the British during the War of 1812.

The Punchbowl

Battlefield Monument

Distance
6 km

Terrain
Rugged, rocky, dirt paths, rail-line crossing, stairs, pavement at Battlefield Park

Location and Parking
77 King Street West, Stoney Creek, L8G 5E5
Large parking lot

Summary of Hike
This is an out-and-back hike to the Punchbowl waterfall using Bruce Trail white blazes and unmarked trails, followed by a loop around the Battlefield House National Historic Site.

1. From the farthest end of the parking lot, with Centennial Parkway on the right, cross the field, walking through a gap in the tree line to continue along a wide grassy path.

2. At the billboard, keep to the right and stay right where the trail splits, crossing over the train track into the woods to continue.

3. At the bridge and white blazes, cross over and continue to follow white blazes through the forest to the access road.

4. At the access road, leave the white blazes, cross the road straight ahead, and go over a small hill. At the landing, take the unmarked path on the right that moves above the creek. (There is a lower trail that

is closer to the creek, on the left side, but it is more challenging.) Continue this upper trail, keeping right as the route moves towards the falls.

5. At the distinct split close to the creek (a high stone peak is on the right), turn left down to the creek. There is a tree on the edge with roots that form a ladder descending to creek level. This allows access to the creek-bed. When it's dry or water levels are low, it is possible to continue into the bowl. This is the turnaround point.

6. To complete the hike, retrace the route back to the access road and follow the white blazes to the bridge. From the bridge, keep right on the unmarked trail to cross the rail line and continue through the meadow near the billboard. Keep left and left again to reach the field and parking lot.

7. Walk through the parking lot, or through the field past the washroom building, towards King Street. Keep right to reach the historic buildings.

Route Map

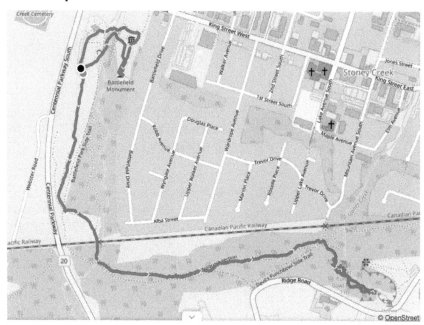

Features and Information

Named for the Ball brothers, who settled in the area in the 1780s and built a grist mill, flour mill, and lime kiln at the lower waterfall. This became an industrial centre in the early 19th century. Many of the buildings have been restored, offering visitors a glimpse of the past. The lower falls plunge 25 metres into Twenty Mile Creek. The layered walls surrounding the waterfall are a composite of limestone, dolostone, shale, and sandstone. Equally impressive is the 11-metre-high Upper Falls, a 1 km hike upstream.

Goat Greeting at the Farm

Upper Ball's Falls

Distance
7 km

Terrain
Some hills, short roadside section, forested trails, some uneven footing.

Conservation Area trails have easy footing.

Location and Parking
Fifth Avenue, Vineland, L0R 2C0
Bruce Trail on east side of Victoria Avenue

Parking is allowed on private property, on the short laneway next to Fifth Avenue

43.14234^0 N, 79.39078^0 W

Summary of Hike
This is an out-and-back hike to the two waterfalls and heritage site. Most of the hike uses the Bruce Trail.

1. From the parking area, walk along the laneway away from Victoria Ave. Follow the white blazes past the farm into the woods, crossing a bridge and dirt road, and continue.

2. At the intersection with the paved road, follow the blazes left along the road and quickly left into the woods, then across a field to Sixth Avenue.

3. At Sixth Avenue, turn left across the bridge and left again into the heritage site, past the chapel and towards the barn. Turn left past the barn to the lookout area for Lower Ball's Falls.

4. Return to the heritage site to explore the buildings. To continue the hike, exit the site near the chapel, cross the road, and walk diagonally across the field towards a footbridge crossing the creek in the Ball's Falls Conservation Area.

5. After the bridge, turn left and continue to follow the trail to the Upper Ball's Falls viewing area on the left. This is the turnaround point for the hike.

6. To return, begin retracing the route down to the first field, and bypass the footbridge to the road. Cross Sixth Avenue to the field on the other side and re-join the white blazes. Continue to follow the white blazes back to Fifth Avenue and parking.

Route Map

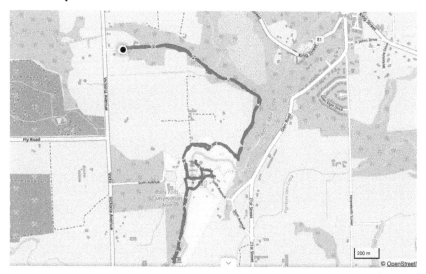

Features and Information

This hike follows the escarpment edge and visits Forty Mile Creek's Upper and Lower Beamer Falls. It also includes the stairs down to the creek's edge to the beginning of the Iroquoia section of the Bruce Trail. A visit to the Gap and an old quarry are added features. This Conservation Area is also famous for hawk watching, especially in the spring. From March to May, naturalists can be found at the Hawk Observation Tower to share their knowledge.

Red-Tailed Hawk

Upper Beamer Falls

Distance
6 km

Terrain
Steep and hilly sections, stairs, some uneven footing

Location and Parking
Beamer Memorial Conservation Area
28 Quarry Road, Grimsby, L3M 437
43.18826° N, 79.57553° W

Summary of Hike
This is a part loop and part out-and-back hike using the Bruce Trail white blazes and side trails blue blazes.

1. From the parking lot, walk down the laneway and along the right side of the field to the corner (observation tower on the left).

2. At the corner, turn right, follow the blue blazes on Grimsby Point side trail. At the intersection with Beamer Falls side trail, turn right.

3. At Ridge Road, turn left. Go over the bridge and keep left to continue inside the guard rail.

4. At the gravel driveway, turn left towards the Boy Scout building and keep left at the trail. Continue the trail towards the creek and falls. There are several small trails leading down towards the falls for a better view.

5. After viewing the falls, turn back and retrace the route over the bridge, turning right onto Beamer Falls side trail to the Grimsby side

trail sign. Keep right, following the blue blazes until meeting the white blazes at a set of stairs on the right.

6. Take the stairs down the ridge. Stay on the white marked trail to the sign on a tree indicating the Bruce Trail boundary of the Iroquoia and Niagara sections. This is the turnaround point.

7. Retrace the route to the top of the stairs and turn right, following the white blazes along the edge and to several lookout areas.

8. Continue following the marked trail until it turns left. Step away from the white blazes briefly to take a short walk straight ahead to view a gap in the escarpment wall. Return to the trail, turn right, and then right again immediately onto a small opening on an unmarked path. Stay right of the fire pit at the bottom of the path to explore the rocks and the quarry.

9. To return, retrace the route to the fire pit. On the right is a short path leading up to the white blazes. At the top of the small hill, turn right and follow the blazes (avoiding side trails) to the field with the observation tower. Keep right around the field, turn right onto the laneway, and return to the parking lot.

Route Map

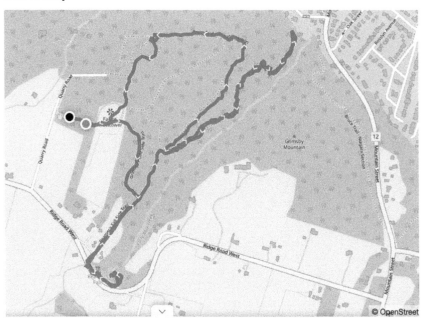

© OpenStreet

APPENDIX: MAPS

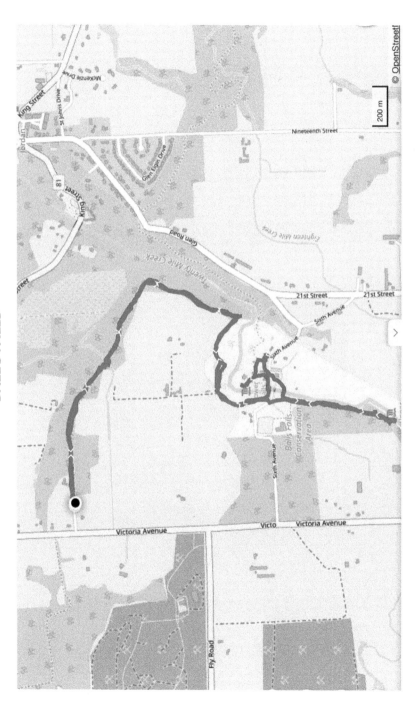

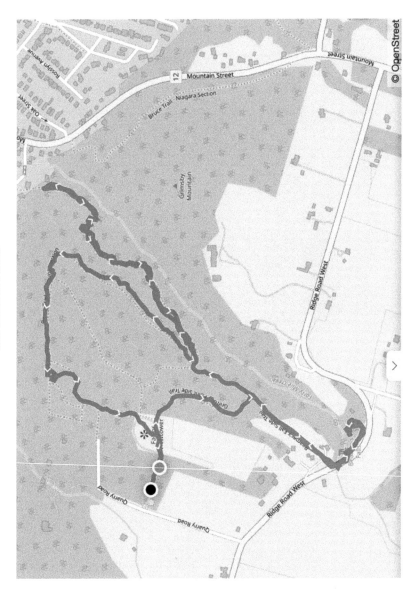

BEAMER FALLS

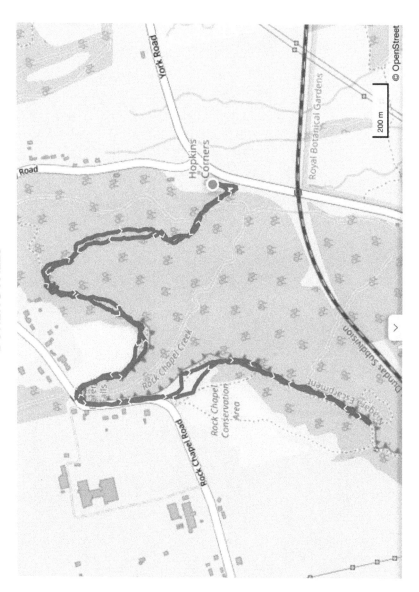

BORER'S FALLS

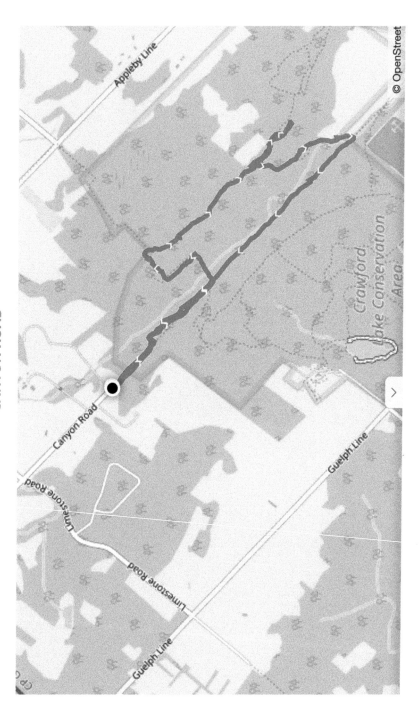

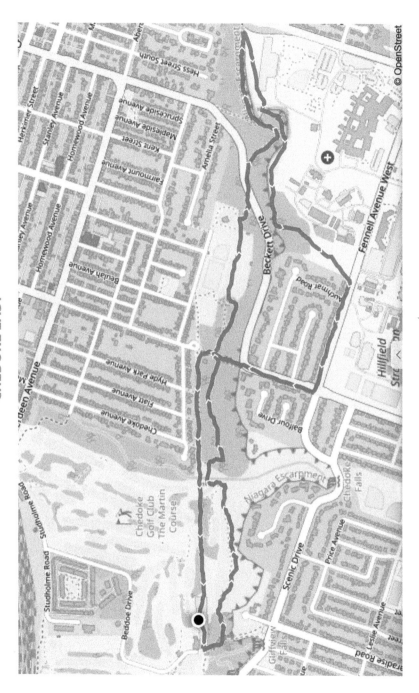

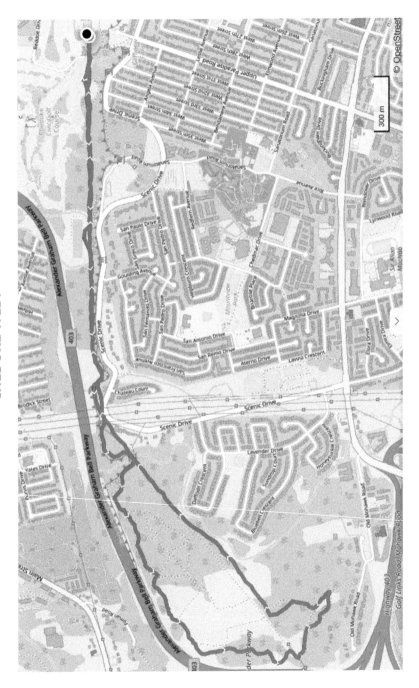

CHEDOKE WEST

300 m

© OpenStreet

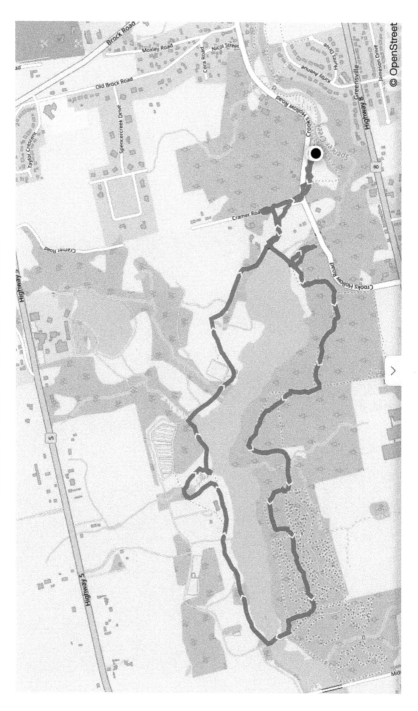

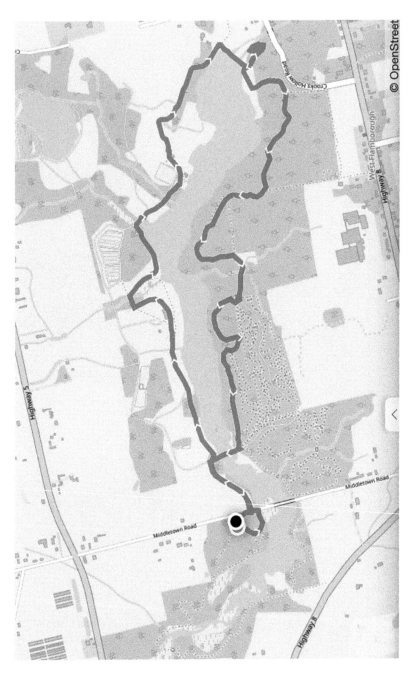

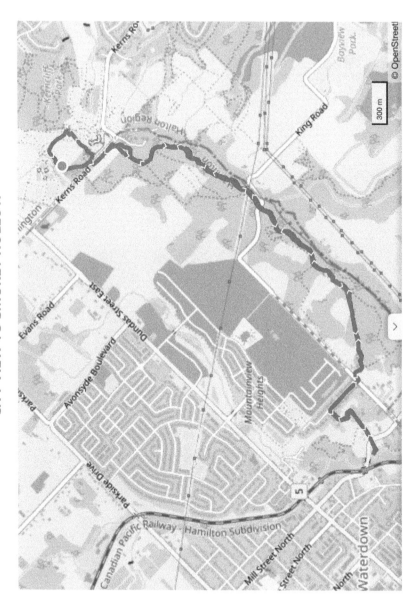

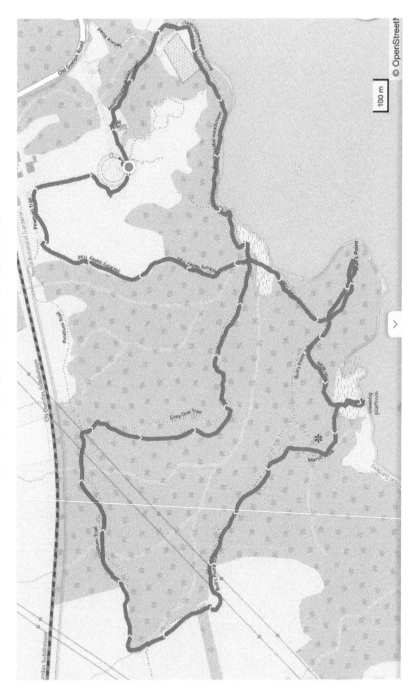

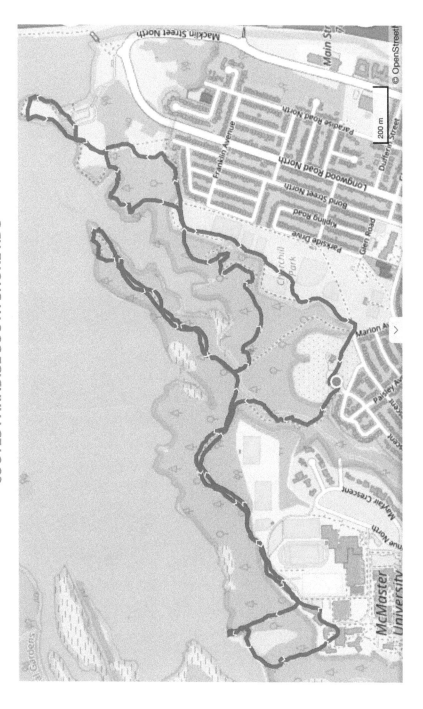

COOTES PARADISE SOUTH SHORE RBG

CREEK SIDE AND MARSHES TRAIL RBG

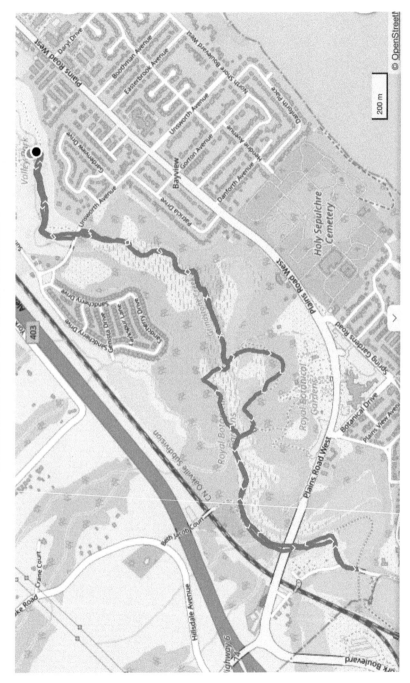

DEVIL'S PUNCHBOWL AND BATTLEFIELD PARK

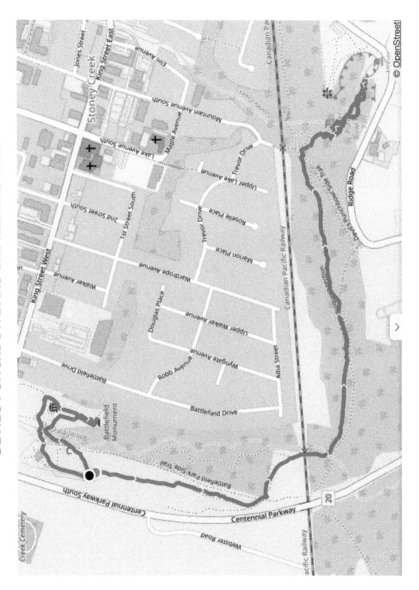

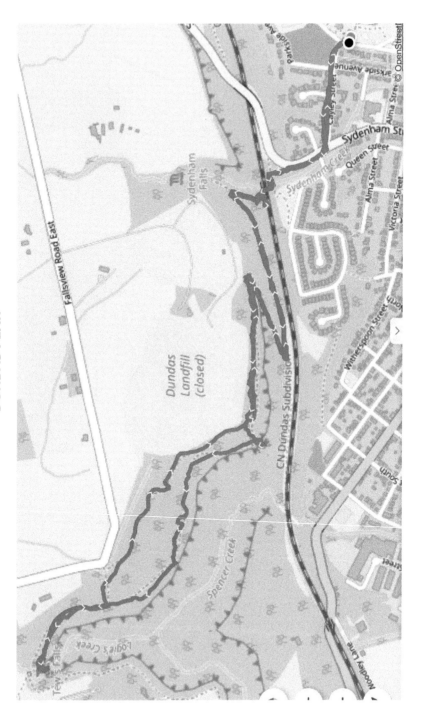

FISHER'S POND

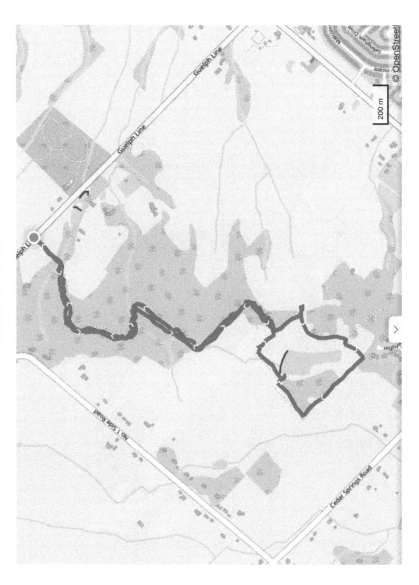

HALTON REGIONAL FOREST

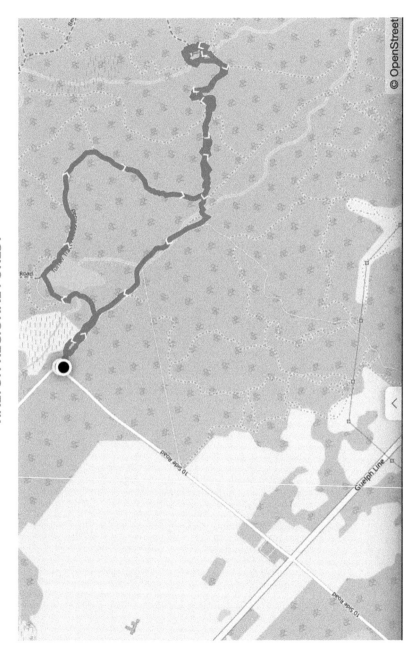

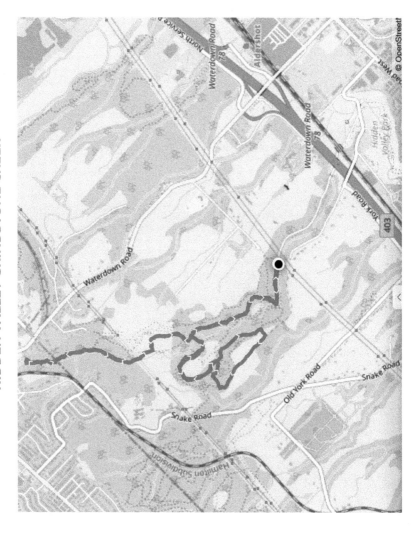

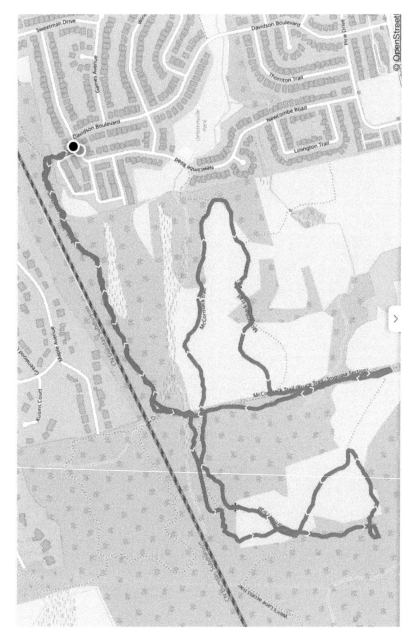

MCCORMACK TRAIL DUNDAS VALLEY

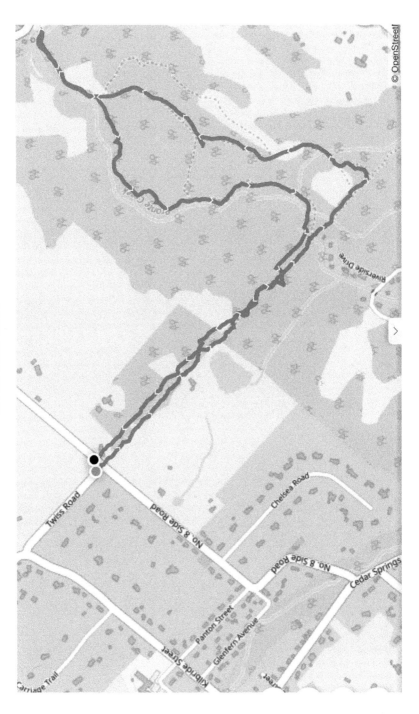

RIVER AND RUIN

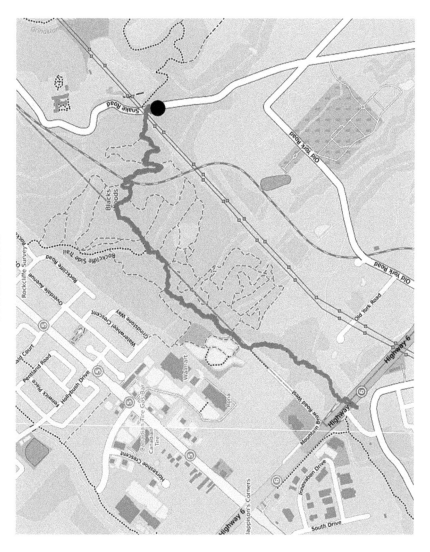

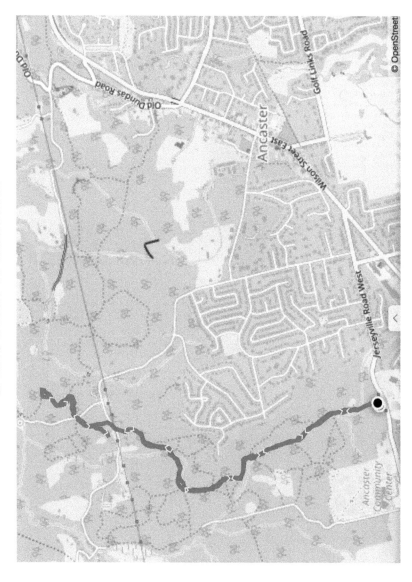

© OpenStreet

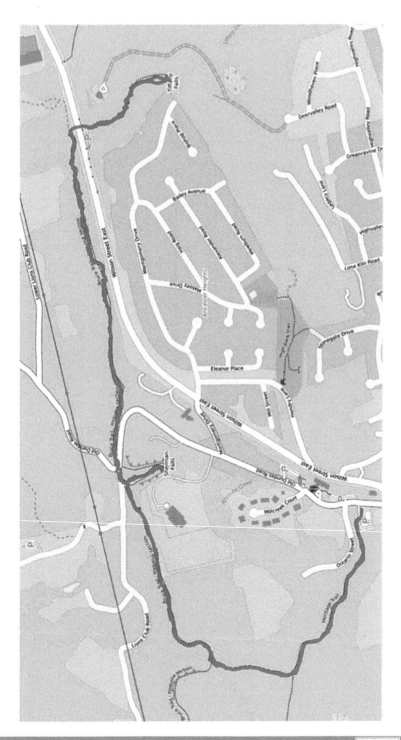

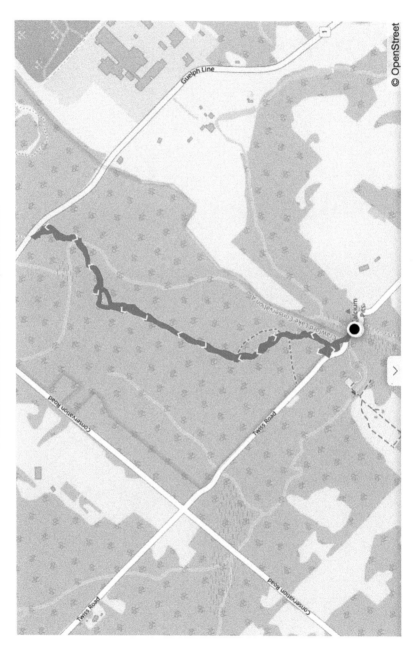

TWISS ROAD EAST TO GUELPH LINE

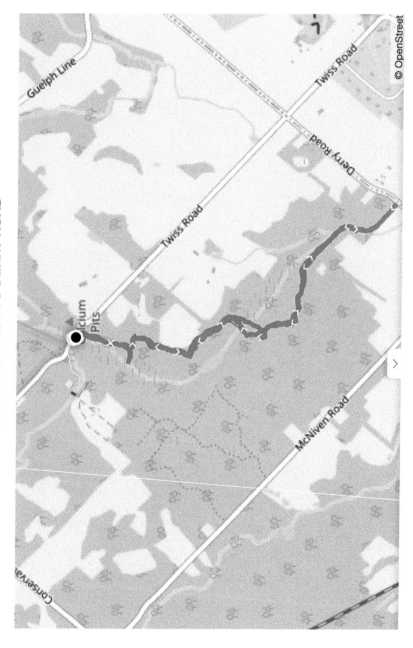

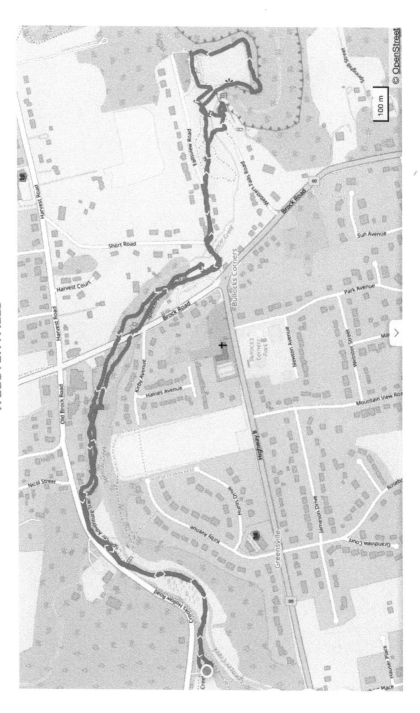

100 m

© OpenStreet

ABOUT THE AUTHORS

Chris Parr and Sharon Tkacz are avid hikers and outdoor enthusiasts, living in the Hamilton and Halton regions. They invite you to follow The Hikers Dozen and share your hiking photos with them on Instagram.
@thehikersdozen